Meditation

The Essential Guide To Meditation For Novices: Techniques For Alleviating Stress, Cultivating Inner Serenity, And Enhancing Well-being

(Comprehensive Manual For Alleviating Stress And Cultivating A Tranquil Lifestyle)

Michal Davenport

TABLE OF CONTENT

What Is Meditation?..1

Establishing The Practice..29

Programs Of Meditation 59

Self-Inquiry Meditation...76

Could You Please Provide Clarification On The Precise Definition Of The Term 'Art Of Blessing'?..81

Your Self-Worth Is Paramount. 91

The Practice Of Meditation................................. 115

Enhancing Spiritual Well-Being And Streamlining Life Through Meditation Practices 126

Engage In A Leisurely Stroll On Your Own Accord. 134

Shedding Negativity 148

What Is Meditation?

The response is rather straightforward - meditation involves engaging in non-action. Meditation entails a state of profound serenity that resonates deeply with the innate longing of one's soul. Allow me to elucidate through the utilization of illustrative instances. What occurs when we experience hunger? Undoubtedly, we experience a strong desire for sustenance and long to consume it expeditiously. Likewise, a similar situation arises when one experiences thirst; the individual yearns for water. Likewise, the essence of one's being propels individuals towards engaging in meditation; succinctly put, meditation serves as nourishment and sustenance for the soul.

As an individual, you assume various roles throughout your lifetime, occasionally becoming entrenched in one of these roles. That instills a sense of discomfort within you and stifles your inner being. Meditation is the sole remedy for alleviating this sensation of confinement. Meditation enables one to transcend societal expectations and perceive oneself beyond the prescribed roles of father, son, brother, husband, and other such designations. Meditation cultivates serenity, tenderness, fondness, and compassion, allowing them to flourish effortlessly within you, gently permeating your inner being.

Meditation facilitates the cultivation of positive mental states, facilitating the elimination of negative thoughts such as anger, worries, and anxiety. Consequently, it enables individuals to embrace a more gratifying existence. This is the exact rationale behind the paramount importance of incorporating meditation into one's existence. Individuals who engage in the practice of meditation are consistently characterized by their unwavering display of positive energy and a composed state of mind.

What are the benefits or justifications for engaging in the practice of meditation?

If you have reached the stage of adulthood, you would undoubtedly have observed the dynamic and energetic nature that life tends to present. Reflect upon the period of your adolescence, or potentially even a time preceding it. Did your perspective on life mirror your current viewpoint? The answer, as you will come to comprehend, will be an unequivocal negative. Have you pondered extensively on the reasons behind its functionality? The primary reason for this increasingly prevalent pattern is centered on the shift in your concern from worldly matters to pursuing activities that truly bring you joy, thereby eliciting a sense of happiness within you.

During your youth, you enjoyed a considerable degree of autonomy, allowing you to engage in a wide range of activities as you pleased. You engaged in leisurely activities with your companions, derived pleasure within the educational institution, and savored each instance of existence. That propelled you towards a state of contentment. Nevertheless, as you matured and embarked on your collegiate journey, or perchance when you commenced your initial professional endeavor, you became cognizant of a pervasive feeling of constraint or discontent. Gradually and consistently, you began to experience the intensity of the job.

Despite the absence of such information, it is highly plausible that you encountered challenges within your relationship and experienced health-related matters, among other potential difficulties. However, there is a prevailing similarity among all individuals who reach maturity and reach their late twenties or beyond; they inevitably encounter various challenges and obstacles. Adults consistently appear to be in a perpetual state of discontentment, while young children invariably exude joy. The distinction lies in the fact that young children act in accordance with the desires of their inner essence, rather than conforming to societal influence. When one exercises restraint over the impulses of their heart, each instance imparts a sense of mounting pressure and discontent, culminating in the cultivation of detrimental characteristics like anger, concerns, and unease. Subsequently, this trajectory propels an individual towards a diminished level of happiness, perpetuating a self-reinforcing cycle. Through the implementation of meditation techniques, one undergoes an alterative cycle, namely that of experiencing joy.

Meditation facilitates the elimination of extraneous distractions from one's life, thus enabling a heightened concentration on the favorable elements of one's existence. In contemporary society, our lives have become incredibly fast-paced, to the extent that our mental faculties often overpower our physical well-being. As a result, even during attempts to rest and sleep, our minds continue to race with incessant thoughts, thwarting our ability to achieve a peaceful state of slumber.

Engaging in the practice of meditation would be beneficial in conquering this obstacle and enabling you to regulate your cognitive processes and mental faculties, thereby affording you the ability to cease activity when unnecessary.

Meditation revitalizes the mind and fosters enhanced problem-solving abilities. Therefore, whether one is confronted with health challenges, financial difficulties, interpersonal conflicts, occupational stress, or any other adversities, the practice of meditation empowers individuals to effectively confront and address these issues. Engaging in the practice of meditation will bestow upon you a renewed mental clarity, affording you the opportunity to embrace a life imbued with profound contentment and satisfaction.

Meditation Postures

Posture constitutes a crucial foundation within the practice of meditation. Indeed, when the term "meditation" is brought up to a group of 10 individuals, approximately 60% of them will likely conjure an image of an individual assuming the lotus posture, with crossed legs and both feet resting upon the opposite thigh.

If any individual among them happens to engage in meditation, it is probable that they will contemplate their meditation environment, the advantageous outcomes they attain, or the emotions they experience as a result of their practice. Proper body alignment constitutes a crucial element of meditation practice, albeit not the sole cornerstone.

It entails more than simply assuming a seated position on a chair or cushion and engaging in one of the prescribed meditation postures. It necessitates more than merely adopting a stance. Without the intention of meditating, that then translates to just a normal posture.

Proper alignment of the body is crucial during the practice of meditation due to the following reasons:

- Participants have the opportunity to experience relaxation and prevent fatigue throughout the sessions.
- Proper bodily alignment enables the practitioner of meditation to experience

a state of ease and stillness for a duration of 10 to 20 minutes.

• The body's functionality is improved by adopting a proper posture. For instance, the maintenance of proper posture ensures that an individual's spinal alignment remains straight, thereby optimizing the efficiency of nerve transmissions.

Nonetheless, proper body alignment poses as a significant challenge for numerous novice practitioners of meditation. Given that numerous meditation postures entail the folding of one's legs (such as the quarter lotus, half lotus, full lotus, Burmese position, and others), individuals who have not been engaging in regular physical activity or those who have a larger body size often encounter difficulties in assuming any of these positions in a comfortable manner.

However, through consistent practice, individuals of any ability can develop the necessary capability to engage in physical exercise and adopt any of the aforementioned meditation poses.

Fortunately, assuming a seated position is not the sole posture suitable for meditation. Meditation can be practiced in various postures, including standing, reclining, walking, or seated on a chair. Of all the available postures, the supine position is the least advised due to its tendency to induce drowsiness.

The proper alignment of the body presents an initial obstacle, but through advancement, individuals gain the ability to adapt and explore alternative postures. Furthermore, individuals have the option to select the most optimal posture that they can consistently adopt. The optimal posture is the one that facilitates a state of calmness, attentiveness, and relaxation, ultimately leading to the attainment of one's desired outcomes. As an individual, you have the option to choose and alternate between two or three different postures.

Components of an ideal body alignment

There exist diverse methods of assuming a seated position during the practice of meditation, namely sitting upon a chair, utilizing a bench, adopting a straddle stance atop a cushion, and engaging in distinct postures that involve crossing the legs. Experiment with various poses and evaluate your comfort level and ability to attain desired outcomes.

In instances of discomfort, it can be readily observable that distractions arise, hindering one's capacity to concentrate effectively, consequently causing a shift of attention towards the various sensations or discomforts being experienced.

The subsequent factors ought to be taken into account when selecting the optimal meditation position:

• Ensure that your spine is in a state of relaxation • Ensure that your spine remains in a relaxed state • Confirm that your spine is in a relaxed condition • Ensure that your spine is free from tension

• Ensure that your posture maintains an erect spinal alignment

• Ensure that your shoulders are gently retracted and in a state of relaxation.

• Provide support to your hands by placing them either on your laps or on a cushion, allowing them to maintain a state of relaxation.

- It is imperative to ensure that your jaw, tongue, eyes, brow, and face remain in a state of relaxation.

- Maintain symmetrical alignment of your head, slightly retract your chin, and ensure that your neck is extended, elongated, and in a state of relaxation.

- It is essential that no body part exhibits tension.

- It is ill-advised to exert oneself in order to sustain a pose, be it due to feelings of discomfort, exertion, or pain. Nevertheless, for individuals who are in the initial stages, it may prove to be quite challenging.

Complimenting your posture

To attain optimal comfort, kindly perform the following actions:

- Adopt suitable attire: it is advisable to don relaxed and appropriately fitted garments whilst engaging in meditation. This facilitates proper respiration without any undue effort. Wearing garments that are excessively tight and ill-fitting will hinder your ability to sit comfortably, causing discomfort and potentially leading to fatigue.

• Avoid excessive food intake: it is preferable to meditate on an empty stomach rather than with a feeling of being overly satiated. Alternatively, consume food in moderation in order to ensure optimal physical comfort while assuming your preferred bodily stance.

• Ensure warmth: in the event that you reside in a region with cold temperatures, ensure that the room is adequately heated. The frigidity of the environment can give rise to a sense of unease, thereby depriving you of the essential solace you require.

Illustrations of meditative positions "Pictorial representations of meditation poses "Demonstrations of various meditation stances "Evidences of different meditation postures "Illustrations depicting meditative bodily arrangements"

There exist several postures that one may experiment with when initiating a meditation practice, eventually selecting the one that best suits them.

- The quarter lotus

- The half lotus position • The half lotus posture • Assuming the half lotus stance

- The entirety of the lotus position

- The stance of the Burmese nation • The viewpoint upheld by the Burmese government • The official position taken by Burma

- Performing seiza (kneeling, either on a zafu or with the aid of a bench)

- Utilize a seat

- Lying down

"Additional factors to take into account regarding body positions are:

- Determining the optimal seat height • Choosing the most suitable seat elevation • Deciding on the ideal seat level

- Identifying the optimal position for your seating arrangement • Assessing the most suitable angle for your seat • Evaluating the ideal inclination for your seating position • Examining the optimum angle to position your seat

- Optimal meditation positioning for the alignment of your head, shoulders, and hands. By taking this approach, you will possess the capability to adjust and control your posture in order to attain your intended outcomes.

As demonstrated previously, a variety of meditation postures are available for adoption. Nonetheless, amid the assortment, the enduring factor remains the pivotal role of the brain. Scientists elucidate that during the practice of meditation, numerous neurological processes occur within our cerebral cortex. For instance, research has demonstrated that during the practice of meditation, there is a notable decrease in the cognitive processing speed of the brain. Scientists elucidate that the manifold benefits we derive are attributable to alterations in the neuronal architecture. In addition to the challenges related to the physical posture, training the mind poses a significant task for any neophyte in meditation. Given that our cognitive faculties are perennially engaged, barring instances of slumber, it proves arduous to channel our thoughts into singular pursuits. Fortuitously, the practice of meditation goes beyond mere cerebral engagement and serves to enhance and refine the functioning of our minds.

Benefits of Meditation

Meditation enhances one's ability to exert influence over the outcomes experienced. The lens through which reality is perceived is your mental faculties. Meditation bolsters mental fortitude and confers an enhanced capacity to exercise discernment in determining one's susceptibility to the influence of reality.

Meditation enhances one's ability to effectively manage the challenges of everyday life. It facilitates enhanced access to one's internal reservoirs while promoting detachment from stressors and other stimuli that diminish one's well-being.

Meditation enhances your self-discipline. By bolstering your resolve and cultivating emotional regulation, you will enhance your ability to make informed and prudent choices and exhibit more effective behaviors. You will discover a heightened ease in overcoming negative tendencies and maintaining steadfast dedication. Additionally, it diminishes your reliance on vices like alcohol and cigarettes.

Meditation sharpens your intellect. A widely acknowledged advantage of practicing meditation is its ability to dispel falsehoods and illusions. This assertion holds true not only in the realm of metaphysics, but also in the conventional understanding. Meditation enhances one's cognitive clarity, facilitating a more rational analysis of situations.

Meditation enhances one's efficiency. It alleviates your mind of diversions, enabling it to operate optimally. Consequently, your attention, recollection, ingenuity, and ability to handle multiple tasks are likewise enhanced. It also facilitates the development of cerebral tissue, enhancing concentration, emotional equilibrium, and reducing vulnerability to cognitive decline.

Meditation energises you. There exist specific meditation techniques intended to impart energy, yet engaging in meditation in any manner elevates one's personal potency. Numerous elements can diminish one's inner resilience, including detrimental convictions, fixation on thoughts, and unfavorable emotions. Engaging in meditation severs your connections with these distractions, allowing for a greater reserve of personal energy to be at your disposal.

Meditation toughens you up. This should not be misconstrued to suggest that mediation induces a sense of callousness and indifference. What this implies is that it enhances your resilience against the issues that previously caused you distress. Engaging in regular meditation enhances your comprehension of the inner workings of your mind, subsequently granting you the capacity to maintain a state of tranquility amidst distressing circumstances. This leads to a more effective recuperation from adversity.

Meditation makes you kinder. Engaging in meditation facilitates a deep self-awareness that subsequently enhances your ability to comprehend and empathize with others effortlessly. It facilitates the ability to disengage from personal concerns and gain insight into alternative viewpoints. Due to the increased level of control you possess over your responses, you no longer engage in defensive mechanisms to protect yourself against the shortcomings of others. Furthermore, a multitude of individuals have come to the realization through the practice of meditation that they share an inherent interconnectedness with all beings and the surrounding world. Consequently, the cultivation of benevolence and acceptance becomes an unescapable outcome for them.

Meditation enhances one's social interactions. By cultivating empathy and fostering greater tolerance, you will enhance your ability to establish harmonious relations with others. Furthermore, you will effectively manage interpersonal connections.

The practice of meditation enhances self-affection. One becomes increasingly compassionate and accepting towards oneself as one attains a state of inner tranquility. The embracing of oneself enhances one's sense of self-assurance, thereby facilitating the organic process of authentic self-expression.

Meditation elicits favorable emotional states. Meditation makes you relax. Inducing relaxation prompts the activation of the parasympathetic nervous system, thereby eliciting positive sensations. The state of bliss frequently arises as a consequential outcome of engaging in meditation. It further reduces instances of negative emotions. Over time, your levels of anxiety, irritability, and sadness diminish gradually. Individuals may hold a greater inclination towards you due to the pleasantness experienced when in your company.

Meditation has the potential to benefit one's overall well-being. Numerous ailments can be attributed to the presence of stress and tension. The practice of meditation can counteract these factors and restore your overall sense of wellness through inducing relaxation and tranquility. In particular, it can help reduce pains, normalize blood pressure and heart rate, relieve muscular tensions, treat insomnia, strengthen immune function, decrease inflammation, and rejuvenate cells.

Meditation has the potential to unveil new discoveries. Meditation enhances your consciousness, enabling you to gain valuable insights that were previously inaccessible. Indeed, numerous instances of psychic occurrences during meditation have been documented, and a consistent practice of meditation serves as a means to cultivate and enhance psychic capacities. Nevertheless, it is imperative not to allow one's focus to be diverted by hallucinations during the practice of meditation. The objective of this activity is to sustain your concentration on a designated objective for a specified duration. Kindly take note of your observations and attend to them subsequently, once your current tasks are completed.

Meditation promotes enhanced presence. Consequently, this enables individuals to allocate a larger portion of their attention towards the present circumstances, ultimately resulting in heightened satisfaction and productivity.

Engaging in meditation can bring one into a closer communion with the Divine. Engaging in meditation can bestow upon you profound, spiritual encounters, such as attaining a heightened sense of direction and establishing a connection with a higher entity. Deep contemplation is also purported to be among the avenues by which one may achieve enlightenment and emancipation.

As evident from the aforementioned, engaging in meditation yields valuable returns commensurate with the time and effort invested. In times of stagnation, it is imperative to recollect the reasons behind your decision to engage in meditation, make necessary adaptations to facilitate a more manageable experience, and subsequently attempt anew. The subsequent chapters will provide comprehensive guidance on the necessary steps to initiate a successful meditation practice and attain proficiency in the discipline.

Establishing The Practice

Although the specific outcomes of individual meditation sessions hold less significance compared to the overall impact it has on one's life, the practice itself can be highly invigorating and motivational. Similar to how physical fitness is attained and sustained through consistent physical activity and a well-rounded nutritional regimen, the enduring benefits of meditation can only be attained through consistent and disciplined practice. Commencing with a disciplined regimen and inculcating advantageous patterns of posture, breathing, and the like right from the outset greatly enhance the pursuit of meditation. These elements bear equal significance to the selection of techniques, as analyzed in Chapter 4.

The objective, nonetheless, is to avoid reliance on a fixed protocol. Contrarily, once a consistent practice of meditation has been established through systematic and scheduled sessions, the ability to engage in meditation will be conferred independent of location or temporal constraints.

Where to meditate

Similar to the serene and tranquil atmosphere experienced in a finely adorned temple or church, wherein individuals engage in prayer and deep reflection, a designated area within one's abode, having been carefully conceptualized and arranged, possesses the potential to evoke a comparable impact, serving as a catalyst for meditative practices.

Select a serene and agreeable location that guarantees freedom from commotion, individuals, or any other forms of disturbances. An optimal arrangement, if feasible, entails allocating a dedicated space, be it a whole room or a designated area within a room, exclusively for the purpose of engaging in meditation. Frequent the same location consistently, particularly during the initial phases - the attachments and ambiance that develop will facilitate the seamless transition into a state of meditation whenever you occupy that spot. In the event that noise is an issue, the utilization of earplugs can prove advantageous. In the event that circumstances allow, the greater your comfort, the more effortlessly you will be able to focus on your practice, fostering a higher probability of your continued commitment to it. Please dress in lightweight and comfortably fitting garments, and kindly remove your footwear.

Creating an environment that exudes simplicity and aesthetic charm can facilitate the process of attaining a reverential state of meditation. Consequently, dedicating attention towards enhancing the aesthetics, whether through visual or sensory means, in your chosen space for meditation, becomes a worthwhile endeavor. Refrain from using intense lighting - opt for natural light or dim, diffused lighting, as these contribute to a more calming ambiance. Certain individuals prefer to engage in meditation in the absence of light or with the gentle illumination of a candle, as such conditions facilitate their introspective focus.

It is imperative to bear in mind the sentiments of one's cohabitants while setting up a designated space for meditation. The use of candlelight and burning incense can effectively establish an ambiance and evoke desired emotions. However, in cases where cohabitation with an individual who experiences allergies to incense or lacks understanding and appreciation for meditation is a factor, it is advisable to approach your meditation practice with minimal disruptions or external elements. In any event, it is imperative to ensure that no form of assistance in meditation becomes essential. Should you find yourself incapable of meditating without the presence of a specific object, image, or other accessories, it is essential to discontinue this dependency. The practice of meditation ought to result in the attainment of internal liberation rather than fostering increased reliance.

Optimal timings for engaging in meditation and determining an appropriate duration

Determining specific hours for meditation is not necessarily imperative; however, it is generally advisable to devise a feasible schedule upon commencing the practice of meditation and endeavor to adhere to it, while maintaining a healthy balance and avoiding excessive fixation on it.

Ideally, it is recommended to engage in meditation twice daily for a prescribed duration. Sunrise and sunset are widely regarded by numerous educators and established practices as the most optimal moments for engaging in meditative practices. Early morning is, indeed, an opportune period for the majority of individuals. Upon awakening, one's mind tends to be comparatively lucid, whereas subsequently, it may require some time to shift focus away from the affairs and concerns of the day. Other opportune moments to consider are prior to your evening repast or prior to retiring for the evening, as long as these time slots align harmoniously with your familial and everyday schedule. It is ill-advised to engage in the practice of meditation immediately following a meal, regardless of the specific time or times you may opt for. This is due to the fact that the body is actively occupied with the process of digestion, which may lead to a diminished state of mental attentiveness. Please allocate approximately one to two hours of rest after consuming a light meal, and more time after a heavier one. Additionally, kindly ensure that the telephone in the room is either unplugged or taken off the hook. Please ensure that the heating is sufficient and that you strive for maximum comfort by allowing an ample interval between meditation sessions when practicing twice daily.

It is advisable to gradually increase the duration of your meditation sessions, as opposed to establishing ambitious goals that may prove difficult to maintain. Novices are advised to allocate a minimum of 10 minutes and a maximum of 30 minutes for their practice sessions. However, it is preferable to consistently dedicate 5 minutes per day rather than irregularly engaging in longer sessions. Do not be concerned if there seems to be a lack of visible progress - the mere act of maintaining a static position for a predetermined duration carries inherent advantages. Therefore, adhere to your chosen duration by remaining seated or reclined. Maintaining diligent timekeeping may not be conducive to the practice of meditation. However, by establishing a consistent daily meditation schedule, one will gradually develop a natural synchronicity with their body's internal rhythm, rendering the dependence on timekeeping unnecessary to signal the conclusion of the practice. Until you become accustomed to discerning the passage of time, it is advisable to position a clock within close range or arrange for the activation of an alarm - preferably one without a jarring audible alert, or alternatively, dampened by the use of cushioning material - as a means to indicate the conclusion of your meditation session.

Meditation Exercises

When you embark upon the initial stages of meditation, it is advisable to avoid placing excessive expectations upon yourself. Developing the ability to mentally disengage from the demands of daily life poses a greater challenge than anticipated. Each one of us encounters circumstances that give rise to concern, each individual has significant matters that require their focus, and undoubtedly, there is always something deserving of our time and attention on which we deem it necessary to act.

A crucial aspect of acquiring proficiency in meditation lies in the recognition and acceptance of this fact. However, it is equally important to acknowledge that the time dedicated to meditation carries inherent value and should not be perceived as squandered.

Once you begin to experience the constructive impact that meditation has on both your mental and physical well-being, you will gain the capacity to relinquish the detrimental thought patterns that urge you to cease your contemplative state and engage in more productive activities. Through dedicating a mere 15 to 20 minutes each day to the practice of meditation, a revelation awaits you: heightened productivity, increased accomplishment, and reduced levels of stress that surpass any previously experienced.

It is advised that you refrain from succumbing to anger or disillusionment in the event that unwelcome thoughts infiltrate your consciousness. It is a universal experience. Merely recognize and subsequently redirect your attention towards your breath, mantra, or any other focal point, persevering in your practice.

Engaging in various meditation techniques can prove beneficial in identifying the most suitable approach for individual practitioners. It is possible that you derive pleasure from the various alternatives available, and depending on your specific objectives, you have the flexibility to select and employ the appropriate choice in each instance.

Additionally, it is worth noting that there is no prescribed duration for meditation. It is important to bear in mind that meditation is a means to enhance your well-being, and hence you should engage in a practice that aligns with your personal comfort. An approximate duration spanning from fifteen to thirty minutes every day is generally suitable for the majority of individuals. However, some individuals prefer to engage in meditation sessions lasting an hour or even longer, while others find ten-minute sessions to be beneficial. It is recommended to explore and experiment with different durations to determine what best suits your needs and preferences.

The sole recommendation I can provide regarding this matter is that you allocate a specific period for engaging in meditation. Do not attempt to fit it in haphazardly within your spare moments on the schedule, as such an approach is unlikely to yield desirable outcomes. Your attention will be absorbed by monitoring the clock, generating unease regarding excessive time consumption, and rendering it impracticable to unwind.

Please find listed below a range of exercises that will assist you in delving into your inner self, comprehending your physical body, and identifying the most suitable meditation techniques tailored to your unique needs. Please feel at liberty to experiment with these elements and infuse them with your individual personality.

Commence every meditation session by implementing the grounding technique, incorporating the exercise of engaging and disengaging the chakras while purifying them simultaneously. With consistent application, this method will become inherently ingrained and intuitive, enabling you to effortlessly transition into a state of meditation with greater expediency.

Following every meditation session, it is imperative to allocate a brief period, ideally one to two minutes, to engage in a state of tranquil repose. This respite allows for the seamless reintegration of one's cognitive faculties into a state of complete conscious awareness.

Acquainting oneself with one's physique

Go into basic meditation. Develop an attentiveness to your breath, beyond mere concentration, actively engage in perceiving and experiencing it. Is it too fast? Is it too heavy? Are you engaging in controlled, rhythmic respiration, or are you experiencing rapid and forceful inhalation and exhalation? Acquaint yourself with the sensation and discern the distinction between your serene inhalations and those laced with stress or anxiety. In which region of your body can you perceive the sensation of respiration – the abdomen or the thorax? How does it feel? Engage in the deliberate control of your breath, ensuring it maintains a measured and consistent tempo.

Once you have regulated your breathing, you can redirect your attention towards your physical being. What are the emotions that you are currently experiencing? In which part of your physical being do you experience that sensation? Do you experience a sensation of nervousness or anticipation in your abdominal region? Do you feel sick? Are you experiencing anticipation or joy? Are you angry?

Acquire knowledge of the bodily sensations associated with these emotions. Attempt to recollect an instance that evoked sadness within you and discern the presence of that emotional sensation. Likewise, it is important to bear in mind emotions such as anger, happiness, joy, and love.

Examine and acknowledge the impact each emotion has on your physical being.

Develop the capacity of your mind to recognize these sensations and embrace them, subsequently redirect your attention and persevere.

You might be questioning the rationale behind my suggestion to subject yourself to emotional turmoil, considering that meditation is intended to cultivate serenity and equilibrium in the body. The reason is simple. By acquiring knowledge about your physical and mental states, you will begin to identify any latent concerns that could be impacting you. Frequently, we possess the perception that we are effectively managing prevailing emotional challenges, whereas in reality, our conscious awareness is inadvertently fixated upon them.

By acquiring knowledge regarding the nuanced alterations in bodily vibrations brought about by these emotions, you will effectively manage them while engaging in meditation or discern them as warranting your attention at a later time in the day. Failure to perceive these alterations during the initiation of a meditation session will result in an incomplete realization of its utmost advantages.

Extending your senses

Go into basic meditation. This exercise has been meticulously devised for the purpose of enhancing your mindfulness concerning your immediate environment during the process of meditation. The essence lies in maintaining awareness of your surroundings and discerning any external alterations that may transpire during the practice of meditation, rather than solely focusing on them.

This is attributable to the fact that when you are in a profoundly concentrated state of meditation, you are not attentively aware of any external occurrences. In the event of an emergency, how would you discern it? By cultivating attentiveness to your surroundings, you will perceive any nuanced shifts in the ambiance and have the ability to respond accordingly, should the need arise.

Execute this activity in a manner consistent with the exercise involving familiarization with your own physique. Augment your sensory perception and perceive the ambient temperature of the surroundings. Is there any draughts? Is it too warm? What is your perception of the atmospheric warmth on your skin? Do regular ambient sounds exist? How would you describe their audio characteristics - are they characterized by being loud, quiet, relaxing, or repetitive? What is the odor/vaporous quality present in the room? Do you perceive any agreeable aromas in your vicinity? Does it exude a scent that is pleasant and crisp, or one that is stagnant and earthy? Do you perceive any odors emanating from the food or the fragrance of flowers? What is the perceived magnitude of the room, does it have a sense of confinement or is it characterized by ample space? Can you please inform me about the current status of the door, whether it is open or closed?

Engage in this activity across multiple rooms on varying days in order to develop the ability to discern disparities in dimensions, temperature, and other factors.

In the event that you can ensure an absence of interruptions, please leave the door ajar and request the discreet presence of your partner or an acquaintance to enter the vicinity, remain there momentarily, and subsequently depart. Did you perceive the distinction when you ceased to be in solitude within the confines of the chamber? How was it different?

If you are able to diligently acquire proficiency in these initial two exercises, you will undoubtedly observe a notable enhancement in the efficacy of your subsequent meditation sessions. Nonetheless, should you find yourself unable to accomplish this, please do not be disheartened. Throughout the course of your existence, you have dedicated significant efforts to training your mind in order to identify that which is readily apparent and dismiss whatever falls outside that realm. Hence, it is entirely expected that your senses will necessitate further cultivation. It requires a considerable amount of time and dedicated effort, and individual accomplishments are attained at varying paces. With persistence and dedication, you will eventually achieve your goal.

Outdoor Meditation

Implore the expansion of your sensory faculties. Locate a tranquil and cozy outdoor location, then proceed to engage in fundamental meditation techniques.

Utilize the methodologies that you have honed through the 'Extending Your Senses' practice and employ them to examine an outdoor environment. As time elapses, you will gradually observe an expansion of your range outward, enabling you to discern subtle variations that lie at a greater distance from your current position.

Visualization Meditation

This exercise centers around the utilization of one's imagination, as implied by its name. This form of meditation can prove highly effective in managing stress and achieving a state of tranquility for the mind. Additionally, research has demonstrated its potential benefits in mitigating symptoms of depression, anxiety disorders, and disturbances in anger regulation. Frequently, visualization meditation, also known as path-working, is facilitated by a guide; however, there is no impediment to employing this technique independently and achieving satisfactory results.

Commence by engaging in fundamental meditation techniques. After achieving stabilization of your respiratory patterns, proceed to mentally envision yourself residing in an environment that elicits a sense of security and solace. Frequently, I opt for the serene ambiance of woodland areas adorned with rushing rivers or a rustic chalet nestled upon a tranquil cliff, affording a picturesque panorama of a nearby shoreline.

You have the freedom to choose any location you desire and curate your surroundings according to your preference. Should you happen to encounter any distractions, do not fret, as it may require a significant amount of time to maintain your focus effortlessly. Just regain your composure by centering your attention on your breathing, and return to the most recent point of recollection in your visualization.

Take cognizance of your surroundings and the tasks at hand. Embark on a journey of exploration and limitless possibilities, allowing your thoughts to guide you to newfound discoveries. The subconscious mind frequently operates during the process of visualization, giving rise to situations where one may encounter challenges that necessitate attention in life, yet are met with hesitation to acknowledge.

Through the practice of visualization, individuals are able to transport themselves to a state of security and ease, wherein their subconscious mind will discreetly provide indications of the challenges they must confront. This approach is deemed effective as it enables individuals to overcome challenges without direct confrontation, allowing for the careful analysis and subsequent realization or decision-making process without the emotional turbulence associated with addressing matters in a tangible manner.

In my personal experience, there have been numerous instances in which I have encountered situations that have left me feeling perplexed and apprehensive. Upon the conclusion of one or two path-working meditations, I have acquired an inherent comprehension of the most appropriate course of action to take. As a result, my anxiety has dissipated, leaving me with a distinct trajectory to follow. Curiously, it was only during the meditative practice itself that I possessed a rudimentary realization that I was effectively addressing these matters.

Should you so desire, you have the option to avert your attention from any familiar allusions and instead relish the experience of immersing yourself in your imagination. Allow your thoughts to guide you and observe where your journey concludes.

The third alternative entails self-guidance. If there is something that needs to be released, one should direct oneself towards a stream, river, or another form of flowing water source.

Retrieve a small stone from the adjacent river shoreline and direct your mental concentration towards the act of bidding farewell to that which requires parting words. This may encompass a range of factors, such as stress, anger, financial issues, interpersonal connections, and any other sources of negativity. Envision the complete permeation of the substance into the solid structure, and thereafter retract your limb and project it with utmost force into the body of water.

Once you have reached a state of readiness, reorient yourself to your physical being and the environment surrounding you, thus concluding your meditation session.

Focus Meditation

Focus meditation involves granting your mind the freedom to wander in whatever direction it desires. Certain cultural and belief systems employ this technique in the practice of scrying, which involves extracting significance from discernible symbols present within elements such as a flame, water, or a mirror.

Engaging in such an activity provides an effective means of honing one's ability to maintain undivided attention and concentration by solely focusing on a single objective.

Please take a comfortable seat and prepare yourself for a foundational meditation practice. Kindly ignite a candle, being sure to place it securely in a location where it cannot topple.

Regulate your breathing and direct your attention towards the illumination emanating from the candle's flame. Do make an effort to refrain from fixating your gaze unwaveringly on the candle, as doing so will solely lead to diversion. Simply remain calm and observe the mesmerizing movement of the flame, allowing your thoughts to wander freely.

Mantra Meditation

You are presented with two alternatives for engaging in this particular form of meditation. One may opt to recite a mantra purely for the purpose of attaining concentration, or alternatively, select a mantra tailored to address any specific requirement at a given moment.

If the intention is to enhance concentration, initiate the foundational meditation and subsequently divert your attention from breathing towards vocalizing your mantra. It is not necessary to perform this task audibly; if desired, you may carry it out mentally. Nonetheless, in order to enhance your concentration and vigor, it is more effective to have an audible stimulus to engage with.

Maintain a consistent and moderate vocal tone, preferably characterized by a subdued pitch, without descending to such a low level that necessitates excessive focus. Ensure that the mantra remains synchronized with your respiratory rhythm. A single-word or two-word mantra to be continuously repeated with each inhalation and exhalation. Extended mantras must be synchronized with the pace and cadence of your breath.

When employing original expressions, it is important to consider certain factors while strategizing your choice of verbiage.

Please ensure that your statement is a constructive affirmation of your desired outcome. Your cognitive faculty does not register 'I will' or 'I want' as a directive. Instead, opt for phrases such as 'I am'.

It is advisable to succinctly articulate affirmations while maintaining a precise focus.

Please make certain that the propositions you put forth adhere to the constraints of physical feasibility. It would be futile to state, "I am going to run a marathon," if one lacks the physical ability to do so. Instead, it would be more appropriate to express, "I am going to enhance my physical fitness."

Ensure that your mantra remains focused on your objectives.

The efficacy of mantra meditations stems from the concentrated direction of both personal life energy and the universal energy towards a specific objective. If you generalize your mantra you could find yourself with some very unpleasant consequences. For example, if you wish to improve your financial situation and you are not specific you could say something along the lines of 'I am going to get a large influx of money.

By omitting the source of this information, you are leaving it up to conjecture and speculation. Consider the emotions that would arise if someone were to pass away and subsequently bequeath an inheritance to you. I am not contending that this would unequivocally be attributable to your actions, however, regardless of the extent of your indirect involvement, you would bear liability for the fatality. This illustration is somewhat exaggerated, yet effectively conveys the gravity of the matter.

Alternatively, one may express it as 'I intend to augment my income through constructive means.'

The following are a few illustrations of mantras that can be employed to bring about positive transformations. You are welcome to tailor them according to your requirements.

To alleviate stress: I am drawing in soothing energies while expelling my feelings of stress.

To facilitate sleep: I have attained a state of inner tranquility and will experience a serene period of rest during the night.

To alleviate anger: I relinquish my anger and embrace love into my essence.

To alleviate discomfort: The intensity of my pain gradually diminishes with each subsequent breath I take.

For the preservation of my dignity and affection: I possess admirable qualities and deserve to receive love.

It is evident that these affirmations possess a positive and uncomplicated nature. Consider your desired outcome and concentrate on it when formulating your speech.

Another benefit conferred by positive affirmations in the form of a mantra is that your mind will become aligned with the words. Similarly to how a melody from your previous years can elicit emotions and recollections, when you silently utter the words to yourself at any time of the day or night, your mind will form a connection between the words and the emotional state you experienced while contemplating your mantra. While engaged in a state of deep contemplation during the recitation of your mantra, you will likely discover that simply uttering the words will facilitate the restoration of tranquility to your mind.

Programs Of Meditation

FIRST PROGRAM - Mindful meditation with a focus on regulating the breath.

1. In the tranquil setting you have selected for contemplation, assume the proficient posture you have acquired. Assess the state of the muscles and alleviate any superfluous tension. Please shut your eyes and direct your gaze toward the floor, focusing on a point approximately 1 to 1.2 meters away from you.
2. Inhale and exhale while using nasal respiration, followed by a brief moment of pause. Respiration ought to be effortless and innate. Feel your breathing.
3. With every exhalation, recite to oneself the word "simply."
4. In instances where intruding thoughts divert your focus from the act of breathing, proceed to conscientiously and promptly redirect your attention back to your respiration, ensuring that you resume uttering the word "just" during exhalation. Continue for 10-20 minutes.
5. My respectful request is that you refrain from rising promptly upon the completion of the session. Please maintain a state of stillness,

by assuming a seated position and keeping your eyes closed. Maintain attentiveness towards your thoughts, emotions, and physical sensations. Please maintain the current course of action, while ensuring that you remain vigilant for the next few minutes.

6. Engage in this exercise routine five to seven times weekly for a duration of four to six weeks.

7. Utilize these alternatives for the activity:

a) Attempt to engage in a practice of numerating consecutively while expelling air from your lungs, beginning with the number one and continuing up to ten, subsequently repeating this process from one to ten once more. In the event that you are unable to maintain a accurate count, I would recommend commencing the enumeration anew by stating "1, 2," and continuing in a sequential manner. etc;

b) During inhalation, mentally instruct yourself to "breathe", and while exhaling, remind yourself to "exhale".

c) Observe the breathing pattern without numerical enumeration or fixation.

thoughts "breath" - "exhale".

Please refrain from excessive concern regarding the efficacy of your meditation practice. This level of anxiety contradicts the principle of adopting a passive approach; it is essential to allow oneself to naturally embrace relaxation at its own pace.

SECOND PROGRAM - Engaging in meditative practice with the utilization of a repeated mantra.

1. Mantra refers to an amalgamation of sounds, words, or names that are consciously recited numerous times as a part of meditation. The mantra serves as the focal point of concentration, thereby facilitating the practice of meditation.

Certain teachers of meditation assert that it is imperative for each practitioner to employ a specific mantra, as it possesses distinctive benefits and facilitates the cultivation of a propitious state of mind. Several studies have demonstrated that randomly selected nonsense words, when repetitively uttered, yield equally effective results as the purportedly "special" mantra. In the traditional application of laya yoga, the fundamental phonemes of the Sanskrit language are utilized, comprising of composed clusters of sounds ng, ant, NIS. Employing these particular sequences of sounds as mantras, devoid of comprehensible significance, may proceed as follows: ANT, thump, Wang, Dang Jang...; ING, Bing Wing, gnng, Jing...

Empirical evidence suggests that any word that holds appeal to an individual can serve as a suitable mantra, examples of which include "peace," "love," "calm," "harmony," and "silence." Additionally, traditional Eastern mantras such as "Om," "Aum" (meaning "I am"), "Soham" (meaning "I-it"), and "Ca-ham" (meaning "I-it") are commonly utilized.

Choose words that resonate with you as your personal mantra.

2. In a tranquil setting that you have designated for the purpose of meditation, assume the appropriate position and observe the relaxation of the muscles, with particular attention to the muscles of the chest and neck.

3. Speak aloud your mantra. Maintain a moderate level of noise (to prevent excessive stress) and avoid overly forceful or vigorous movements (to minimize the risk of hyperventilation and dizziness).

If articulating the mantra audibly poses a challenge, recite it internally within your mind. When distracted by alternate thoughts, redirect your focus back to the chosen mantra. As time progresses, you will establish for yourself the most suitable cadence for reciting mantras, thereby facilitating profound relaxation.

4. After the passing of approximately 5 minutes, transition to the practice of softly uttering the meditation mantra. Through sustained meditation, one becomes

increasingly attuned to the rhythmic nature of the mantra, leading to a deepening state of relaxation.

5. It is recommended to engage in this exercise for a duration of 15 minutes per day, ideally 5-7 times every week for a span of two weeks. Subsequently, you may consider prolonging the duration of each session to 30 minutes. By the conclusion of the initial week, under optimal circumstances, you shall possess the capability to momentarily expel all matters from the realm of your consciousness, save for the mantra. Engage in deliberate meditation and focus intensively on the mantra for approximately one month, subsequently determining whether to incorporate this practice into your meditation regimen.

6. Rather than engaging in mantra meditation, you can explore an alternative variation of this practice. After carefully choosing your designated meditation posture, diligently and repeatedly visualize the chosen word, serving as a mantra, with deliberate slowness in the realm of your imagination. Allow your hand to perceive and exhibit the word.

7. Once you have gained proficiency in focused breathing meditation and mantra-based meditation, you can merge and integrate these practices together. To initiate the posture, commence by directing your attention to the

act of respiration: inhale at this junction, followed by exhalation, and a brief suspension of breath at this juncture. Proceed with this practice for a duration, refraining from any deliberate attempts to regulate the pace of respiration. Once one reaches a state in which the act of breathing happens inherently, incorporate the chanting of the mantra. Please perform the action on the exhalation.

3
A Meditational Prayer
A Glimpse of Existence

What is the outcome if, at any point, we cease to respire? Simple. We will die. It is imperative that we engage in the act of inhaling, taking in breath, and subsequently exhaling, expelling breath.

It is crucial to engage in contemplation of the entirety of the Lord's Prayer. Furthermore, proceed to invert the prayer and return to its initial point. Jesus said,

"Inquire, and your request shall be granted; explore diligently, and you shall discover; make a persisting effort, and the portal shall be unlocked before you" (Matthew 7:7 GNT). I came to realize that I was actively seeking and supplicating to God, thereby hindering my own personal and deliberate engagement in the comprehensive process of acquiring the necessary knowledge and skills to independently address my needs. I found myself in a situation akin to Adam's in the Garden of Eden—when faced with adversity and the need for personal responsibility, I tended to shift blame onto others. The fruit was given to me by the woman you set beside me, and I partook of it. We blame others. We blame evil. We blame the system. We blame the devil. We hereby disclaim any responsibility for our involvement.

If I exhibit a single act of trust and dedication, God will reciprocate with twice the measure of support and assistance. The absence of actions renders faith lifeless. In the context of the Lord's Prayer, the phrase alludes to the Father's intention to bestow blessings upon individuals, contingent upon their active participation in the process. Maintain unwavering belief and diligently carry out the tasks at hand. I am available to provide assistance and guidance throughout the entire process.

Prayer and meditation constitute a fundamental aspect of one's existence. It necessitates adopting a way of life that involves inquiring, searching, and persistently requesting. It is imperative to undertake this activity within a secluded space dedicated to deep contemplation and devout introspection, while maintaining a state of complete tranquility.

By engaging in contemplation of the Lord's Prayer, it becomes deeply ingrained within the recesses of our minds and the core of our souls. It becomes an integral component of our being. It resides within us, and we are incapable of evading its influence, as it emerges as a beacon, a detailed plan leading us towards our redemption. We come to realize that our foremost pursuit lies in seeking the sovereignty of God and his righteousness. It is akin to the individual who unearthed the valuable asset within the parcel of land. Subsequently, he proceeded to divest himself of all possessions and proceeded to acquire that parcel of land.

I pondered frequently whether it was feasible for certain individuals to engage in prayer for extended periods without reiteration. According to popular belief, prayer denotes the act of engaging in conversation with God, whereas meditation involves maintaining a state of stillness and attentiveness in order to listen to God. Meditation involves consciously inviting a sense of sacredness and spiritual connection by seeking solace and entering a state of heightened awareness. This requires stillness. In a state of tranquility, the vocal utterances are emitted. In days gone by, I would often encounter the proverbial phrase passed down by the elderly, stating that "All that you are seeking to comprehend is within your immediate grasp, just beneath the tip of your nose."

There exist multiple techniques and designations pertaining to the practice of meditation. An approach to meditation entails the practice of focusing one's attention and engaging in deep reflection. To engage in concentration, one may engage in the practice of attentively monitoring one's breath or engaging in deep contemplation of passages from holy texts, musical compositions, or specific thoughts. There exist numerous publications and instructional courses dedicated to the practice of meditation. I am inclined to concentrate on the breath.

The divine bestows upon us the precious blessing of respiration. Deprived of respiration, existence would be unattainable. Directing our attention towards the breath enables us to reside in the current moment, abstaining from contemplating the past or the future. During the process of directing attention toward the breath, it is common for the mind to frequently deviate from its focal point. The objective is to cultivate mindfulness of any instances where the mind tends to stray, and then gently redirect one's attention back to the breath. With increased practice, an earlier realization of your awareness will be achieved, enabling you to redirect your attention towards the breath. You will commence perceiving the emergence of thoughts in your consciousness. You will come to realize that your attention has shifted away from your breath. I refer to this as shutting the door in your closet and exercising vigilance towards any subsequent opening of the closet door. The objective is to remain grounded in the present moment, exhibiting complete mindfulness without engaging in any cognitive attachments to it.

One acquires comprehension, discernment, and sagacity sans the presence of prejudice or apprehension. It could be articulated as follows in a formal tone: "One may approach this as an exercise in cultivating mindfulness towards the intrusive nature of the fleshly mind during moments of anticipation for a connection with one's Christlike consciousness, and developing an attunement to the subtle inner voice that communicates without audible sound."

In the year 1991, during my tenure as a chaplain at Walter Reed Army Medical Center, I made it a regular practice to frequent the hospital chapel on a daily basis. I would allocate a duration of forty-five minutes to engage in a focused meditative practice centered around the twenty-third Psalms. Furthermore, I frequently engaged in jogging sessions within the premises of Rock Creek Park, where my primary attention was directed towards the recitation and contemplation of the twenty-third Psalm.

While in the confines of the hospital chapel, I accessed a rejuvenating source of vitality within. I surmised that this is the essence of the psalmist's sentiment. I gradually realized that the Bible emphasizes internal contemplation rather than external preoccupation. I comprehended and acquired knowledge that the realm of God resides within. I am cognizant of the existence of a wellspring within me, and such a reservoir is accessible within the depths of every individual's soul.

The Almighty has bestowed upon us the precious gift of sustenance in the form of living water, the bread that nourishes our souls, and the radiant light that guides our way through life, residing deep within our beings. Irrespective of our respective colors, races, financial backgrounds, or educational achievements, it holds no significance. In order to reach the destination, it is imperative to adhere to the path of righteousness, as described in Matthew 7:14 in the King James Version. The privilege to access such blessings was granted to me through the combination of my genuine sincerity and unwavering persistence, the divine grace and mercy bestowed by God, and the assistance of the Holy Spirit.

Prayer and meditation constitute the essential spiritual practices that sustain both the Church and every individual within it. I earnestly pray and aspire for my personal voyage and comprehension to positively impact and inspire others, impelling them to commence or persist in their own journeys in accordance with their guiding spirit. Additionally, during the state of meditation, the ethereal entity that communicates without producing audible vibrations conveyed the following: "What is presently classified as myth was once regarded as an indisputable verity, and what is presently considered truth shall be denounced as fallacy in the future."

I contemplate the significance accorded to Greek Mythology, as well as the recognition bestowed upon the Greeks and Romans for their pioneering role in the exploration and advancement of various disciplines." It is worth noting that the ancient Greeks embarked on journeys to Africa, specifically Ancient Kemet. During these travels, they acquired knowledge which they subsequently incorporated into their societal, educational, political, and religious frameworks.

Africa, historically known as Kemet, held a prominent position as a center of advanced knowledge, thus it can be asserted that the Greeks derived their knowledge from our predecessors. The narrative of Ausar (Osiris),

Aset (Isis), and Heru (Horus), which we refer to as a myth, was comprehended as such in the region of Cush (Ethiopia) a millennia ago, approximately 10,000 years in the past. However, "Johnnie come lately" interpreted them as actual living people and missed the truths within the myth.

Anthony T., a renowned scholar specializing in the history and cultural contributions of African-Americans. Browder, during his discourse on the origins of Christianity in the Nile Valley, alluded to various factors when questioned about the historical process of Egypt's invasion and subsequent usurpation. According to his statement, "The spiritual essence embedded in our myths became overshadowed as our people began perceiving them as tangible entities." The populace gradually succumbed to the allure of materialism." I comprehend now that this progression has been an ongoing reflection of our decline. I will continue to contemplate the concept that what is considered a myth in present times was once regarded as truth in the past, and what is presently acknowledged as truth may eventually be deemed a myth in the future. We are currently residing in an era of change, wherein the biblical text will increasingly be recognized as a collection of folktales, symbolic narratives, and mythical depictions representing the spiritual principles of ancient Egypt.

Please allocate some time to peruse the literary work titled "The Destruction of Black Civilization" authored by Chancellor Williams. I recollect an instance wherein my wife (Natalie) and I forged a friendship with an Orthodox Jewish Chaplain due to the discrimination he was encountering from certain members among the chaplaincy. He informed me that a revered rabbi conveyed to him that "his community, in fact, ventured into Africa and engaged in acts of violence and appropriation, effectively taking over the Jewish heritage and attributing it to themselves." According to both Browder and my professor of ecclesiastical history, the Catholic church subsequently established its authority in the African temples, initiating a process of cultural co-optation. One could argue that the structures commonly referred to as Jewish temples could also be classified as African or Cushite temples, if we so choose.

As a collective, we have endured numerous instances of having our identity systematically diminished and subsequently conditioned to resist any means of reestablishing our connection to said identity. As we embark on our homeward journey in order to establish connections, we will disregard and denounce the signs and symbols that come our way, deeming them malevolent, diabolical, or heathen, and retreat to the place where we have been conditioned to remain, while others freely engage with our possessions. Dr. William E.B. DuBois possessed an understanding of this concept. This statement was eloquently articulated by the author in his renowned literary work, "The Soul of Black Folks." It highlights the notion that once an individual's mindset is effectively influenced and manipulated, there is no longer a need to be concerned about their subsequent behavior. It is unnecessary to instruct him to remain in this location or to proceed to another point. He will discover his appropriate position and will remain steadfast within it. There is no requirement for him to be sent to the rear entrance. He will proceed autonomously, without receiving any explicit instruction. Indeed, in the event of an absence of an existing access point, he will clandestinely create one in order to serve his personal interests. His education renders it indispensable. - W.E.B. DuBois stated, "His education renders it indispensable."

Dr. Carter G. Woodson, the esteemed architect of Black History Week, which is recognized as the predecessor to Black History Month, authored a literary work titled "Mis-Education of the Negro". Within the pages of this profound text, Woodson astutely observed that during his era, our community was subjected to cultural indoctrination rather than genuine education within the American schooling system. I would further broaden this to encompass religious establishments. "He authored a literary work titled "The Chronicles of the African American Church." The catchphrase of the United Negro College Fund is "the intellect is an appalling asset to squander."

Our endeavor must encompass liberating our consciousness from the influence exerted by the colonial powers of the British, French, American, and Vatican City empires, employing us as mere commodities to further a worldwide apparatus of servitude. Hence, it is imperative that we draw upon the rich cultural heritage of ancient Kemet as a guiding influence for shaping our spiritual development and sense of self. If we fail to initiate action from that standpoint, the significance of Black Lives may forever go unrecognized, allowing the intellectual elite to continue shaping the discourse and influencing the social landscape. We need to exercise prudence when European scholars begin interpreting Kemetic history to us.

Our healing framework is anchored in the ancient times, when Rome dismantled our spiritual essence by transforming it into organized religion. For a significant number of individuals, this presents a formidable challenge to undertake and an arduous concept to accept. It challenges the foundations of our conditioning. Not all individuals are obligated (or destined) to ascend the identical peak, nor are all individuals obliged (or destined) to consume the same medication guiding them towards spiritual emancipation.

Self-Inquiry Meditation

This particular form of meditation facilitates the reconnection with one's consciousness, which is typically obscured by an array of thoughts, concerns, burdens, engagements, objectives, aspirations, emotions, and cravings.

One of the key factors contributing to the efficacy of this meditation is the opportunity it presents for individuals to delve beneath the surface of their thoughts, fears, worries, and other mental states through engaging in a self-inquiry process. Through this investigation, gain a deeper understanding of the ways in which your thoughts, beliefs, habits, sentiments, and other aspects of your being are shaped. exert an impact on your emotional state, overall welfare, physical condition, and well-being.

"Allow me to present a method by which one may engage in the practice of self-inquiry meditation:

How to

"To engage in the practice of self-inquiry meditation, please adhere to the provided instructions:

Step 1

Transition into a suitable setting for meditation with the objective of engaging in mindful practice for a predetermined duration that aligns with your personal comfort level. Assume a relaxed stance, commence the timing mechanism, either shut your eyes or maintain them unobstructed, unwind and reestablish a connection with your breath; moreover, you may anchor your attention to the immediate physical state.

Step 2

Once you experience a greater sense of tranquility and stability, incorporating breath mindfulness meditation into your initial meditation routine is advisable in order to aid in this process. Subsequently, commence the practice of open monitoring and attentiveness towards the flow of thoughts entering and departing from your conscious awareness. Unless a thought is repetitive, should it be the case, one may engage in meditative contemplation of said thought, but otherwise it is prudent to refrain from fixating one's awareness on any specific thought; rather, one should cultivate an intimate awareness of the transient nature of one's thoughts.

Step 3

After engaging in a dedicated period of open monitoring, it is advisable to sustain awareness of one's stream of consciousness, specifically identifying the objects of the mind's fixation. However, upon the emergence of any thought, it is recommended to subject the thought to scrutiny by employing pertinent inquiries, such as examining the essence and characteristics of said thought. To whom does it rightfully pertain?" Archetypal inquiry into the origins of this notion, and analogous interrogations that stimulate profound introspection and contemplation.

Step 4

It is to be expected that your mind will naturally seek to analyze your thoughts. Although this tendency is not inherently negative, it is advisable to cultivate an intention to simply allow your thoughts to exist without an excessive focus on analysis. Instead, strive to be consciously aware of the process of self-inquiry. The more profound your level of awareness, the more enhanced your intuitive capabilities shall become. Approach your thoughts with an unbiased mindset.

Continue to practice meditation in this fashion, maintaining a mindful awareness of thoughts as they arise and dissipate, refraining from actively participating in any of them, throughout the entirety of your meditation session.

Through the adoption of this technique of attentively observing the mind's tendency to engage with predetermined thoughts, and subsequently redirecting its focus towards the observation of the cognitive realm, a heightened state of detachment from one's concept of the SELF (the "I"), as well as the assortment of beliefs utilized to filter life experiences, concerns, anxieties, and incessant rumination, shall be cultivated.

Could You Please Provide Clarification On The Precise Definition Of The Term 'Art Of Blessing'?

From one perspective, it can be argued that the primary aim of the world is to revive and strengthen our inner faith in God. The initial and paramount measure an individual can undertake in their quest for a connection with the divine is to attain mastery in the practice of imparting blessings. Should one engage in the deliberate cultivation of the practice known as the Art of Blessing for a modest duration, it can potentially serve as a catalyst for the revival of one's dormant faith in the divine. However, it is only through a steadfast and continuous commitment to this remarkable spiritual discipline that the possibility arises of transcending individual identity and merging harmoniously with the divine entity, thus achieving a state of complete unity with God in all respects. It is our firm conviction that this initiation embodies an exceptional revelation of unparalleled significance to the entirety of humankind, representing a singular existence unrivaled in any corner of the world.

To commence, the only prerequisite is a steadfast belief in the presence of a divine entity, or alternatively, a willing receptivity to partake in the sacred practice of bestowing blessings. This is the sole requisition for the maturation of this "grain" through the praxis of the Art of Blessing, thereby unveiling its resplendence of unparalleled magnitude. Upon achieving a state of profound union with the divine, it becomes evident to us that God encompasses all existence and stands as the sole veritable entity. Upon attaining this state, we achieve a state of unity with the divine. Due to the all-encompassing nature of divinity, when we attain a state of profound spiritual transcendence referred to as Samadhi, our perception is solely centered on the divine essence, leading to a simultaneous temporal detachment from our individual sense of self. By engaging in the practice of bestowing blessings, we come to a profound understanding that instances of Divine Grace are not mere isolated events. They are manifestations of the inherent desires that can be precisely elicited at our discretion through the practice of the Art of Blessing, and they are indispensably requisite manifestations.

The power of benevolence derives from the transcendental energy of the Supreme Divine Entity, and it confers upon us the ultimate favor, which emanates from the Supreme Divine Essence, beyond the boundaries of the three realms (material, ethereal, and transcendental). The profound insights that Sri Yuktesvar attained and imparted to Yogananda, as documented in the book "Autobiography of a Yogi," regarding the nature of divinity, the realms beyond, and the physical, astral, and causal planes, form the essential foundation for comprehending the profound principles that underlie the practice of bestowing blessings.

This article intends to provide an exposition on the concept of the Art of Blessing, delineating its methodology, and elucidating the profound impact it bestows upon both the practitioner and the recipient of the blessing.

The Key to Being a Source of Blessings as an Artistic Individual

By engaging in the discipline of the Art of Blessing, one has the ability to enable the seamless movement of the transcendent Supreme Energy beyond the boundaries of mere existence and non-existence, encompassing an individual. It originates from the all-encompassing domain of the eternal transcendence that pervades the Supreme Being. There exists no celestial entity that can rival it or surpass its magnitude. Its pervasiveness is ubiquitous, having endured since the inception of existence, and claiming unequivocal dominion over all facets across the realms. The adept who attains proficiency in all facets of this methodology will come to the realization that everything in the cosmos is interconnected with the divine entity known as God the Father. This Energy guides us towards the singular and everlasting truth of the eternal divine essence, elucidating the ultimate verity pertaining to the ultimate embodiment of the timeless Supreme Being. The gradual augmentation of the Divine Energy assists us in surpassing Maya, the fundamental origin of both pleasure and suffering, thereby enabling us to lead a life untainted by impurities and characterized by the realization of our utmost potential for benevolence. The Supreme Divine Energy emancipates us from all that restricts us, empowers us to attain divine enlightenment while remaining unswayed by the turbulence of existence, and ultimately brings forth our absolute and unparalleled deliverance. It imparts upon us the knowledge that every individual embodies a divine presence, thereby allowing us to immerse ourselves more deeply and frequently in emotions of affection, empathy, mercy, pacifism, and selflessness. Furthermore, it imparts the message that each individual is an embodiment of the divine essence. It serves as both a driving force and a source of nourishment that propels us towards ultimate liberation from the cycle of reincarnation. It affords us an enhanced comprehension of the essence of the atman. Furthermore, it possesses the capacity to revive within us a boundless and unwavering affection, thereby endowing us with an exceptional reservoir of inner strength.

A genuine sense of modesty and self-denial; the cultivation and enrichment of our childlike essence; the goal of fostering greater selflessness while reducing our ego; the profound recognition of the incomprehensible enigma that is God the Father; the aspiration to magnify our selflessness while diminishing our ego; the profound comprehension that the essence of God the Father remains an utterly inscrutable enigma; the yearning to enhance our selflessness while diminishing our ego; the profound grasp of the ineffable enigma that is the reality of God the Father.

The capacity to exercise one's own volition is bestowed upon us by a divine entity, yet it is incumbent upon us to fully optimize its capabilities. By means of this, we possess the liberty to engage in any desired pursuit, albeit not all desires align with permissible conduct. Through the employment of the Art of Blessing, it is the individual who beseeches God for His benevolence, assuming the role of a proponent, while the ultimate determination of the acceptance or rejection of the proposal resides solely with God. During the sacrament, the level of profound Energy that we acquire through Sahasrara is directly proportional to the extent of diminishment of our egos. The response provided to us entails a methodology for discerning the degree of self-centeredness that most accurately characterizes each individual. It is imperative that we refrain from deceiving ourselves.

The internal impediments encompass: absence of trust in a higher power; excessive concern with one's own appearance, superiority, and conceit; absence of empathy and malevolence; engaging in immoral acts and promiscuity; feebleness, excessive fascination with material possessions; materialistic desires and self-centeredness; cruelty, malevolence, and enjoyment derived from causing pain; intense anger, rage, aggression, and engagement in unlawful activities; disrespectful doubt and mockery; harboring feelings of resentment, envy, spreading malicious rumors, and engaging in slanderous speech; indolence and indifference.

Individuals who do not achieve success in their endeavors to engage in the Art of Blessing should sincerely evaluate which of these obstacles are applicable to their circumstances and strive to discover a resolution to that particular concern. Consistently advocating the matter is of utmost significance, and if pursued with earnestness and conviction, divine intervention shall promptly transpire. In the realm of mankind's quest for spiritual proximity, no obstacle proves unconquerable.

Your Self-Worth Is Paramount.

Self-esteem is widely regarded as a comprehensive concept that encompasses individuals' emotional states. If one were to stumble, certain individuals may observe, 'Madam, this individual appears to possess a diminished level of self-assurance.' Conversely, when one articulates a genuine source of pride or exudes unwavering confidence, others may opine, 'You express an undue degree of self-assurance and it may be prudent to adopt a more modest stance.'

However, in actuality, self-esteem surpasses mere superficiality. In essence, this refers to an individual's subjective assessment of their own worth. Frequently, they articulate their perception of appropriateness and the degree to which they believe they are entitled to various facets of life.

To be more precise, self-esteem can be defined as the confidence one possesses in their own skills and capabilities. It evaluates numerous indicators pertaining to trust, such as B. Their perceived capabilities, the manner in which they ought to be regarded, others' interpretation of them, and the privileges to which they should be entitled.

Individuals who possess diminished self-esteem tend to be commonly perceived in an unfavorable manner. They will hold the belief that they are lacking in value to others and maintain constant communication with one another. As a result, individuals often choose to ostracize others from their existence and detach themselves from the confines of reality. This act serves as a gateway to numerous other complications and conditions, notably including depression and anxiety.

If you happen to experience low levels of self-confidence, you may find solace in idealizing individuals who possess high levels of self-assurance. If your perspective differs, it is possible that you do not comprehend the reasons why individuals do not simply perceive things similarly or cease expressing grievances related to self-pity. Nevertheless, the intricacies of the entire situation are significantly more complex. We trust that this book will provide you with an enhanced comprehension of the mechanisms behind self-esteem and facilitate the identification of your own individual position in this regard.

What Influences Self-esteem?

Maintaining one's self-esteem can prove to be quite challenging. Given that this concept is purely centered around the intersection of neuroscience and religion, specifically pertaining to the contents of one's mind, it becomes challenging to locate and employ contemporary machinery and technology in a manner that adheres strictly to scientific principles.

Nevertheless, through the implementation of therapeutic techniques centered around social skills and manipulative strategies, we can gradually gain insight and influence over an individual's thought processes. By acquiring this valuable information, we can enhance our comprehension regarding an individual and gain a more comprehensive understanding of their narrative. Based on this information, it is possible to ascertain the factors contributing to the manifestation of low or high self-esteem in individuals and assist them in discovering more effective approaches.

Throughout centuries of research, physicians, therapists, and social workers have discerned various recurring patterns in patients, elucidating the factors contributing to individuals possessing exceedingly low self-esteem, as opposed to those who appear to cultivate a profound appreciation for their physical being.

Thanks to modern medicine and access to the information we have now, we can publish these results to the world and (hopefully) teach them about the people and the world around them.

In this setting, we acquire knowledge concerning the factors that impact one's self-esteem.

Herein lies an enumeration of the foremost six factors as perceived by scientists, which are believed to exert an impact on self-esteem, encompassing both negative and positive influences. It is crucial to recognize that they may not be applicable to your particular circumstances. Each individual possesses unique attributes, and endeavoring to gauge one's life encounters and self-worth against others is highly likely to diminish one's self-esteem and undermine the ability to foster self-belief.

The manner in which you were brought up.

Our self-esteem is greatly influenced by the manner in which we are brought up. In our early stages of development, encompassing infancy, toddlerhood, and adolescence, we are highly susceptible to the influences of individuals' aid and way of life. Escort a minor and transport them to a domestic setting where they are compelled to endure hardships in acquiring sustenance and toil for an extensive duration of 16 hours each day to overcome these challenges. It may become apparent to you that it does not possess an inherent sense of value.

However, in the event that you must facilitate the adoption of a child into a household where two caring parents are committed to providing the optimal environment for their children, while simultaneously pursuing personal fulfillment, you may observe that such a child displays higher levels of self-worth and diminished self-doubt compared to a child from a less advantaged background.

As our organization develops, the utilization of positive reinforcement and motivation plays a crucial role. Due to our inherent vulnerability during the early stages of life, the establishment of our sense of belonging and love plays a pivotal role in shaping our future trajectory. Consequently, a significant number of scientists are of the opinion that human interaction and affection, including embracing, amicable kisses, or "ventilation," are among the fundamental elements crucial for the cultivation of children's self-esteem and moral principles.

The individuals who encircle you

The majority of your emotions stem from individuals who accompany you throughout your daily engagements. The manner in which individuals engage with you, your subsequent interaction with them, and the nature of your connection with them significantly influence your perception of yourself.

Consider the following perspective: In the event that you constantly find yourself surrounded by individuals who provide assistance during challenging circumstances, it is imperative that you strive for excellence and commemorate your most remarkable achievements. How do you feel? Now envision a scenario where you find yourself encompassed by individuals who engage in conversation with you merely out of a sense of duty, devoid of any genuine interest or concern for your thoughts. Or maybe they are only free when they benefit from them, and they never seem to give you space in their daily routines. What are your thoughts regarding this particular scenario?

The initial option will enhance your sense of worth and instill a greater sense of security when interacting with others. You are enveloped within a community of individuals who possess genuine concern for your well-being, and you tend to struggle in acknowledging your own intrinsic flaws. To some extent, they validate your presence. Conversely, the second situation may prompt you to scrutinize your association with individuals of such nature. What is the reason for your lack of fondness towards me?" "Why do they not allocate sufficient time for their engagements?" "What actions or behaviors on my part might have led them to distance themselves from me?" Such queries arise in situations where there is an imbalanced dynamic in a relationship. As time progresses, this persistent issue will gradually erode our self-esteem and undermine our self-confidence.

Social Processes

Social processes refer to the mechanisms through which groups and individuals engage, adapt, refine, and establish behavior patterns and relationships via complex social interactions. In the field of psychology, the social process concept pertains to the recurring and common patterns that interactions can assume. Engaging in shared activities and interpersonal exchanges serves as the bedrock of social existence, with such interactions occurring within the framework of social processes.

Social exchanges necessitate reciprocal actions, which are influenced not only by the parties involved, but also by the caliber of their interpersonal rapport. These relationships are present between individuals and individuals, groups and groups, or individuals and groups. As a result, interpersonal communication holds significant value as it contributes to the modification of behavior. In the course of this interaction, the parties involved exert a mutual influence on each other's conduct.

There exist numerous social processes, however, certain ones manifest persistently within the collective of a society. They include:

Attitude

Attitude pertains to the overall assessment an individual forms towards an object, concept, individual, or collective that they have encountered throughout their life experiences. An individual might maintain a viewpoint towards racism, articulating that "Racism is unequivocally unethical." Subsequently, this outlook would serve as a guiding force, shaping the person's conduct, cognitions, and sentiments concerning this matter. A shift in perspective takes place when an individual alters their belief, be it a transition from positivity to negativity, a change from slight positivity to extreme positivity, or a transformation from a lack of attitude to the adoption of one. Researchers have been prompted to investigate the mechanisms underlying attitude changes due to the pragmatic significance of attitudes in an individual's existence.

The Dual Process Framework

This method of attitude modification categorizes the existing research into two primary mechanisms: those that transpire with minimal cognitive exertion and those that necessitate a substantial degree of effort.

The primary determinant of the employment of either minimal or extensive cognitive exertion is contingent upon an individual's capacity for critical thinking and their level of motivation.

Low Effort Processes

When the factors at hand do not adequately address an individual's motivation or when their cognitive capacity is diminished, such as when the person lacks engagement with the current situation or when numerous distractions are present. In the present scenario, the manifestation of this degree of disassociation can be attributed to either basic inferential mechanisms or extensive automatic associative processes.

Associative Processes

The processes of association encompass affective priming, classical conditioning, and mere exposure. Classical conditioning endeavors to induce an alteration in attitude through passive cognitive processes, followed by linking a neutral attitude object with the stimulus. For instance, let's imagine that on every occasion you encountered your aunt during your childhood, she would take you to visit the zoo. Engaging in this experience would foster a favorable outlook towards your aunt. If she deviated from her routine of taking you to the zoo during her forthcoming visit, and instead decided to escort you to the medical practitioner's office for the administration of distressing immunizations, the outcome would be the inverse.

Empirical evidence demonstrates that this procedure yields superior outcomes when conducted using a stimulus of preceding neutrality.

However, notable alterations have been documented in cases where individuals shifted their perspective from positive or negative stances.

Affective priming is characterized by the formation of an association between two stimuli, wherein a negative and a positive stimulus, such as the words hate or love, are presented immediately prior to a new attitude object. In instances like these, an individual's response to the adverse or beneficial stimulus influences the assessment of the subject in question, culminating in a modification of their perspective. For instance, in the event that an individual presents you with a suggestion for a dish at an unfamiliar dining establishment, you approach the experience with an optimistic demeanor, anticipating that the meal will indeed live up to your culinary expectations. A similar occurrence is probable to arise if you find yourself in a dining establishment and are attended to by an aesthetically pleasing member of the serving staff. Your comportment towards the server is likely to shape the comportment you exhibit towards the food. While it is true that one's perception may be influenced by the act of eating, the significance of one's initial positive attitude cannot be understated.

The phenomenon of attitude change can be observed in both affective priming and classical conditioning, wherein the alteration of individuals' attitudes is instigated by the presentation of either a positive or a negative stimulus. Nevertheless, it has been discovered that the continuous encounter with a specific entity devoid of any connection.

As an individual gains increased exposure, their demeanor tends to adopt a more optimistic outlook. This phenomenon could potentially elucidate the reason why a neonate demonstrates a discernible leaning and reaction towards the vocal cues emitted by its maternal figure. It is possible that during the child's prenatal development, he experienced frequent exposure to his mother's speech, resulting in the formation of a strong association between the child's emotional response and his mother's voice. Consequently, this association strengthened the bond between the child and his mother.

Inferential processes

Cognitive balance is regarded as one of the fundamental mechanisms for facilitating attitude change. Individuals attain equilibrium when their preferences align and dissent arises towards their undesired circumstances. Any additional factors apart from that induce uneasiness and compel individuals to recalibrate their attitudes in order to establish a fresh equilibrium. For instance, if you and your former partner share a preference for frequenting the same dining establishment, it is probable that the prospect of encountering them there may engender a sense of unease or discomfort. In order to address the disparity created, it is essential that you modify your perspective and approach, either by acquainting yourself with and developing an affinity for an alternative eatery, or by altering your sentiments towards your former romantic partner.

Attribution is focused on the deductions individuals draw about themselves and others when they observe the manner in which a situation or behavior transpired.

Self-perception is an attitude change that occurs with minimal effort, whereby an individual becomes out of touch with their own beliefs. In this particular instance, an individual deduces their attitude from the conduct they exhibit, similar to how one would do so for another individual. Hence, if an individual is observing a promotional advertisement for peaches, he may deduce that he has a preference for peaches, even in the absence of prior contemplation on the matter. Gaining awareness of this aspect of your character will likely lead to a more favorable disposition towards peaches.

Heuristics can be considered as another manifestation of minimal effort in adjusting one's mindset. It is derived from straightforward decision rules that are predicated on prior observations or experiences. Several instances of heuristics include notions such as "greater magnitude implies superior quality" and "expert opinions are invariably accurate." In situations where individuals possess limited cognitive capacity and lack the inclination to engage in complex reasoning, they invariably resort to relying on such straightforward guidelines, which then serve as the foundation for their evaluative judgments.

One could examine the charts to ascertain the ranking of songs in order to determine the quality of recently produced music. By electing to pursue the most esteemed alternatives, individuals will implicitly endorse the notion that the collective consensus on optimal choices corresponds to the absolute pinnacle. It instills within the individual a propensity to cultivate a favorable disposition towards the music that resides atop the popular music listings, rather than embracing a more discerning approach of personally experiencing the music prior to forming judgments regarding its quality.

High-Effort Processes

These processes necessitate the utilization of one's cognitive faculties to a greater extent compared to the preceding ones. Decisions regarding attitude made within these processes are self-governing and are contingent upon an individual's interests, preferences, and personal inclinations.

The initial factor involves cognitive reactions, whereby an individual's attitude undergoes transformation due to their thoughts and exposure to persuasive messages pertaining to the subject matter.

The second approach involves the use of expectancy-value processes, wherein individuals formulate attitudes based on their evaluation of the likelihood that the attitude object will be linked to favorable or unfavorable values and outcomes. Positive outcomes and principles are influential in shaping positive disposition, and conversely, negative outcomes and principles can lead to a negative attitude.

The third process, known as dissonance, posits that individuals have a tendency to uphold their attitudes. Consequently, it is this inclination for coherence that leads them to undergo unpleasant physiological arousal when they partake in actions that contradict their established norms and beliefs. In this scenario, undesirable physiological arousal may manifest as heightened cardiac activity, perspiration of the palms, and similar bodily responses. The feelings of discomfort compel them to modify their perspectives until they arrive at a single alternative that aligns with their respective systems. In addition to altering one's attitude, discord can also be alleviated through modifying behavior.

The Practice Of Meditation

Preparing for Meditation: Cultivating Physical and Mental Readiness

The practice of meditation encompasses remaining vigilant and focused while maintaining a state of physical relaxation. Prior to commencing your meditation, ensure that you allocate a specific time slot during which you will not be susceptible to disruptions, be it through phone calls or requests from individuals within your familial or professional circles. Choose a tranquil and well-illuminated setting that instills a sense of security and relaxation. Prior to commencing your meditation endeavors, ensure that your corporeal state is alleviated by attending to physiological needs such as visiting the lavatory, hydrating with water, and consuming a light refreshment or substantial sustenance. This measure will serve to inhibit intrusive physical impulses that might disrupt the process of meditation. In order to maximize your comfort while acquiring knowledge about your body and to mitigate the potential distress caused by discomforts, it may also be beneficial to ensure proper cleanliness of your body and maintain moisturized skin.

Please ensure that you are dressed appropriately or make necessary adjustments to the room's temperature to ensure that your body remains comfortably warm or cool. Select a plush seat cushion crafted from a luxurious textile that offers optimal comfort for sitting.

If you intend to incorporate music into your meditation, it is advisable to select familiar compositions devoid of any sudden jarring sounds, unpleasant ear-piercing tones, or abrupt musical passages. Enable the continuous loop feature on your music player to avoid interruptions caused by the need to switch to a different track.

The Proper Stance for Meditation

Although there exists a variety of alternative meditation methods, such as reclining, assuming different seated positions, engaging in gentle movements, and finding balance, the majority of introspective practices traditionally commence and conclude with a fundamental seated posture. This role has the potential to be applied to a range of meditation methods, such as mindfulness, breath-focused exercises, visualization, fixed-point contemplation, devotional practices, and auditory stimulation.

The appropriate seating posture for meditation is of utmost importance as it allows the practitioner to attain a state of relaxation while ensuring proper blood circulation and sustained focus. Remaining attentive is of utmost importance, as the practice of meditation encompasses not only attaining a state of relaxation, but also cultivating a state of mindful awareness.

Commence by selecting a locale devoid of distractions and maintaining a temperature that ensures the utmost comfort. Eliminate all additional sources of diversion, including your mobile device. Please don comfortable attire that is free from discomfort, restricts movement, or applies pressure to your body.

Kindly have a seat upon a cushion placed on the floor. Alternatively, should you desire, you may opt to perch on a sofa, an executive chair, or a mattress, provided they afford you the ability to maintain an upright and unstrained posture.

To accentuate the inherent curvature of your spinal column, assume a posture wherein your legs are crossed before you while sustaining a slight anterior pelvic tilt. Ensure a balanced distribution of your body's weight between both your legs and buttocks. Please take a seat in a chair, ensuring that both of your feet are positioned evenly and firmly on the floor.

It is imperative that your head remains aligned with your shoulders while you proceed to elongate your neck and spine. Please slightly retract your chin. Ensure that you maintain a state of relaxation in your tongue, brow, eyes, and jaw. Ensure that your hips and shoulders are aligned in a relaxed position. In order to expand your chest, allow your shoulders to retreat. In addition, you may consider delicately bringing the soles of your feet in contact with each other, while flexing your knees and drawing your heels towards your pelvis, as a viable substitution for crossing your legs. An alternative option would be to consider embracing the "lotus" position, a traditional meditative posture characterized by crossed legs, with the right foot resting on the left thigh and the left foot resting on the right thigh.

Your hands may be gently conjoined or alternatively, the palms may be positioned in either an upward or downward manner, while you rest your arms upon your lap or knees. Furthermore, an alternative approach would be to adopt a traditional gesture, in which one creates a circular shape using the index or middle finger and thumb, subsequently placing the hands on the knees with the palms facing upward or by flipping the hands over and resting the palms on the knees. Please ensure that you firmly position your hands and assess whether your posture is exerting any undue pressure on your shoulders.

Allow the thoracic and abdominal regions to gently ascend and descend at a pace that is comfortable, while enabling the effortless circulation of breath as it enters and exits the corporeal vessel. In order to prevent excessive stiffness, it is advisable to enable the natural movement of your spine and shoulders in tandem with your breath. Inhale deeply into your thoracic region, allowing the expansion of your chest as you take a few breaths. As you engage in the act of exhaling, allow yourself to progressively relax and unwind, all the while ensuring that you maintain the feeling of an expanding and opening chest. You are now equipped to commence the practice of meditation.

Meditation Exercises

Presented herein are a selection of expeditious and effortless contemporary meditation methodologies that can be readily incorporated into your daily regimen. These exercises are appropriate for individuals who are new to the practice and are of a fundamental nature, thus making them adaptable to various settings such as your residence, workplace, or serene outdoor locations by a water body or in a picturesque garden.

A number of these exercises can be completed within a time frame as short as ten to fifteen minutes daily and still yield advantageous results. As you progress in your meditation practice, it is advisable to gradually increase the duration of your sessions, possibly extending them to an hour or more whenever feasible. Select one or two options that you feel inclined towards and proceed with trying them out.

Practicing Diaphragmatic Breathing: The foundational element in the majority of meditation methods involves the practice of deep, controlled breathing. If you lack prior experience in meditation, commence your practice by indulging in this particular meditative exercise, ensuring repeated sessions until you attain a state of comfort and familiarity. Subsequently, you may consider exploring alternative forms of meditation. Locate a serene and comfortable location at which to commence. Eliminate all additional sources of diversion, such as your mobile device. Arrange a suitable seating posture conducive to meditation. Direct your attention exclusively to your breath.

Please make a mental note of the auditory and sensory perceptions that arise when you inhale, allowing your lungs to be filled with air before it exits your body via your nostrils. Slowly and deeply inhale. Gently redirect your focus towards the fundamental act of breathing when your mind strays to any cognitive distractions. Experience a sense of relief as you embrace the sole obligation of upholding tranquility by observing silence and focusing exclusively on the rhythm of your breath. Continue engaging in this practice until you gradually attain a state of rejuvenation and tranquility.

Musical Mindfulness: Select a serene and undisturbed space for your music meditation, where you can comfortably immerse yourself in the experience of listening to music. Your preferred selection of soothing music should be playing. A considerable number of individuals opt for instrumental music, especially when it incorporates the melodies of nature, chimes, or orchestral strings. Assume a composed and attentive posture while engaging in deep and intentional breathing to induce bodily relaxation and alleviate mental distress and preoccupations. Immerse yourself in the auditory elements of the music by placing focused attention on its soundscape and melodic patterns. When your thoughts begin to wander, redirect your attention back to the music while engaging in deliberate, leisurely breathing.

Positive Assertions: Encounter a setting in which you can unwind and liberate yourself from disruptions. Free your mind from concerns and apprehensions through assuming a meditative sitting posture and engaging in deep breaths until a sense of tranquility is achieved. Reflect upon several positive self-affirmations. You have the option to employ the provided examples of positive affirmation or create unique ones of your own.

Enhancing Spiritual Well-Being And Streamlining Life Through Meditation Practices

With frequent engagement in meditation, the mind attains liberation from chaos, leading to a simplification and reduction of complexities in one's life. "Here are several alternative approaches to cultivate a greater sense of fulfillment:

1. Remove all excess – Engaging in meditation eliminates mental clutter, yet to embrace a more straightforward existence, it is essential to eliminate the superfluous elements in your surroundings as well. Disorder and disarray contribute significantly to increased levels of stress and anxiety. When one's life is characterized by a lack

of clutter, one's mind is similarly devoid of clutter.

2. Refine your concept of achievement – Should you insist on measuring success solely by attaining billionaire status, contentment will perpetually elude you. Revise your concept of success to align with a more pragmatic and less materialistic perspective.

3. Exercise financial prudence - Engaging in meditation assists in suppressing impulses and cravings, enabling one to maintain a lifestyle in accordance with their financial resources. Failing to adhere to a budget will inevitably result in financial liabilities, contributing to significant mental and emotional strain in one's existence. Do not incur financial

hardship in an attempt to make a favorable impression on others.

4. Assimilate the notion of sufficiency - The practice of meditation assists in cultivating a deeper sense of satisfaction with oneself and one's circumstances. One can enhance this skill further by acquiring a thorough understanding of the authentic significance of the term "sufficient". Do not excessively strive for things that are unnecessary.

5. Pardoning - The practice of meditation enhances one's receptiveness to the act of forgiving. In order to enhance your sense of fulfillment and reduce the complexity of your life, it is imperative to relinquish any resentments that reside within your heart. Keep in mind that by extending forgiveness, your life

will be imbued with greater happiness and a sense of fulfillment.

6. Maintain a broad perspective - Your life becomes enriched and more enjoyable when you adopt a receptive attitude Take into consideration the perspectives and viewpoints of others, as they may possess validity and accuracy.

7. Learn t0 Delegate – Do not be a control freak. Delegate tasks to others. This will greatly facilitate your daily existence.

8. Smiling is an indomitable force that can triumph over any pain or stress. When one acquires the ability to relinquish minor concerns and greet adversities with a smile, their existence

becomes more streamlined and enhanced.

Enhanced spirituality is among the numerous advantages that can be derived from engaging in meditation. Through consistent engagement in mindfulness, concentration, and meditation, one aligns oneself in closer proximity to the Divine and the Creator.

Presented below is a meditation technique that can be utilized to cultivate a deeper connection with the divine entity:

1. Assume a position of comfort and gently shut your eyes.

2. Prepare by taking a series of deep breaths, inhaled through your nostrils and exhaled through your oral cavity.

3. Invoke the presence of the Divine by offering a humble prayer of thankfulness.

4. Recite the word "God" as you inhale and exhale. In the event that your thoughts start to stray, redirect your attention towards the term "God." Please allocate a time period of 10 to 15 minutes for the completion of this task.

5. Conclude your meditation practice by offering a brief prayer expressing gratitude.

6. Make it a habit to engage in this regularly.

Keep in mind that prayer is widely regarded as a prevalent technique of contemplation. When engaging in prayer to the Divine and Creator, it is advised not to rely on pre-established formulas and to refrain from making requests. Ensure that the manner in which you engage in prayer exhibits a conversational tone. This practice will enable you to develop a stronger connection with the Divine Power.

Mindfulness is an alternative form of meditation that fosters a deeper connection with the Divine. By cultivating mindfulness and inhabiting the present, one gains the ability to perceive elements that may have been previously overlooked or underappreciated, such as the very air we respire, the exquisite floral manifestations in one's own garden, and the myriad blessings encompassing both material possessions and human connections. By cultivating a state of mindfulness and embracing the present moment, one frequently finds oneself in awe of the divine craftsmanship, leading to a heightened proximity to the Divine.

Engage In A Leisurely Stroll On Your Own Accord.

The natural environment functions as a non-pharmaceutical, side effect-free remedy for alleviating depressive symptoms.

In an ideal scenario, we would endeavor to venture outdoors on a daily basis and fully immerse ourselves in our surroundings. Although some ingenuity may be required, it is entirely feasible for us to accomplish this, even if it is limited to brief intervals.

If the sole opportunity for outdoor activity on any given day is limited to the act of walking to your vehicle in the morning and subsequently returning indoors upon your arrival back home, it would be advisable to maximize this short duration to the fullest extent.

Engage in a purposeful stroll while attentively observing your environment:

the ambient temperature, any detectable scents, the intensity of hues in your surroundings, and the delicate manner in which the breeze interacts with your hair. The trees exhibit a vibrant shade of green, the flower petals possess a delicate and tender appearance, the clouds manifest a substantial thickness, and the luminosity of the light is of exceptional quality. Any minor particulars that you can discern.

If perhaps there are days when your schedule only permits you to slightly open a window and deliberately inhale, in those moments, kindly engage in this practice with awareness. Rest assured that in due course, there will be an opportune moment when you shall have the chance to allocate more of your time to venturing outdoors and engaging in exploration. Engage in the exploration of the natural environment with the innocence and inquisitiveness of a young individual, be it by strolling across verdant meadows or gently caressing the cool cascades of a public fountain. This offers a notable juxtaposition to your everyday regimen, furnishing a modicum of diversity to your mindfulness exercises.

However, one may find that their mind possesses the ability to deceive them into believing that they have an overwhelming amount of tasks preventing them from venturing out, or that the prevailing weather conditions are either too hot or too cold for their preference. Furthermore, individuals may also convince themselves that allocating time for personal rejuvenation would have negligible impact on their overall well-being. We possess a collective aptitude in formulating justifications. Alternatively, you might belong to the category of individuals who thoroughly enjoy venturing outdoors and consistently allocate time for this purpose. However, it is possible that you fail to fully absorb the vast array of experiences that are available to you due to a lack of mindfulness. We venture out to the park while allowing a resounding podcast to permeate our auditory senses. We engage in an aerobic exercise routine; however, our primary concern lies in the prospect of expending calories rather than fully appreciating the magnificence of the captivating sunset unfolding before us, adorned by its resplendent amber-hued clouds.

I enjoy engaging in a mindful stroll outdoors within the confines of my backyard whilst accompanying my canines during the morning hours. We possess a slightly weathered stone pathway situated beneath a cluster of trees positioned on the right side of the dwelling. This pathway commences from the fence at the front of our residence and extends towards the stairs that ascend to our rear entrance. I walk down to the fence and back again, slowly, while watching my feet do their quiet work. Although not a formidable accomplishment in the realm of meditation, I am anchoring myself (in a literal sense) and commencing my day on a positive note through the act of mindful walking. (Amusingly enough, it puts me on the right path, figuratively speaking.)

*

While we are aware of the beauty and therapeutic qualities that nature exhibits, it is important to exercise caution and consideration as we navigate enclosed spaces. It is possible that you reside in a locality where the prevailing climatic conditions or the overall environment present obstacles to one's ability to engage in outdoor activities, or at the very least, hinder one's capacity to derive sufficient enjoyment from such activities, thereby impeding concentration.

During my initial experience as a nurse, my contemplative strolls involved traversing the corridor to attend to my patients on the night shift. There were ample occasions for engaging in mindful walking throughout a shift that extended from 6:45 pm to 7:15 am, rest assured. The soreness in my calves and feet served as evidence of my extensive walking regimen, however, my mind remained restless throughout the night without respite. It was preoccupied with the well-being of others and occasionally overwhelmed by witnessing the burden of pain borne by my patients.

Nevertheless, I developed the inclination to conscientiously endeavor to maintain mindfulness and awareness as I commenced my walk from the nurses' station towards their respective rooms. I was aware of deepening my breath, and felt each step as my black clogs firmly connected with the well-trodden floors. Maintain proper posture with a straight back, relaxed neck, and lowered shoulders. I devoted a period of time to expressing gratitude for my capacity to perform ambulatory movements, recognizing how frequently we overlook the extraordinary nature of this ability. The coherence, equilibrium, and coordinated muscular actions involved as we hurriedly transition from one location to another. I unequivocally experienced an enhanced sense of consciousness and perceptibility on evenings when I diligently made these minuscule endeavors to practice mindfulness. These instances of mindfulness created a sense of expansion within me, enabling me to experience gratitude for my personal well-being and develop a profound admiration for the bravery exhibited by those under my supervision.

*

Develop a novel practice of cultivating mindfulness while engaging in the act of walking. Perhaps while traversing the corridors to access the restroom facility at your workplace, transitioning through entrances, or during leisurely strolls with your canine companion. Ensure to maintain a state of relaxation and as you take each step, consciously sense the firm support beneath your feet. Providing foundation and sustenance, akin to the rhythm of your breath. Appreciate these small moments that have the power to anchor you to stability, serving as a refuge from turbulent thoughts.

Judging our Partners

In contemporary times characterized by a tumultuous and hectic manner of living, our significant others emerge as dependable pillars upon which we can rely. We dedicate a significant portion of our time in their presence within our household and anticipate their comprehension of every issue we share with them. Their comprehension skills fall short of our expectations, resulting in a strain on our relationship with them. The current rise in separation rates can be attributed not only to the gradual liberation and expression of suppressed emotions, but also to the abandonment of longstanding norms wherein individuals remained bound in unhappy relationships. Furthermore, there is a growing tendency to perceive the other person in the relationship through a different lens. The unrealistic demands placed on one's partner, such as expecting them to have identical preferences in literature or acquaintances. It is our desire for them to perceive the world from our perspective.

Our collaborators also consist of individuals hailing from distinct familial backgrounds, endowed with a unique genetic makeup, and nurtured with a set of values divergent from our own. Each system possesses its own unique array of values, belief systems, qualities, and traits that are subsequently transmitted to future generations. Therefore, should there occur a divergence in viewpoints, it is not solely the result of conscious conduct, but rather the influence of a power surpassing individual control. Therefore, in order to enhance the satisfaction and inclusivity of our relationships, it is imperative that we accept both our partner and their familial structure without seeking to change it. We cannot cherry-pick certain aspects and attributes of an individual, and then anticipate the relationship to be satisfactory and whole. In order to achieve success, it is imperative that we embrace it wholeheartedly, encompassing all of its facets. Examining them beyond our conscious perception can assist us in comprehending the intricate complexities that hinder us from experiencing a mutually rewarding partnership.

When individuals enter into matrimony or establish a romantic partnership, the initial phase exudes charm, as it brims with burgeoning affection, newfound joy, and a renewed commitment to open and reciprocal communication. However, over time, all of these elements begin to deteriorate. Our primary objective then becomes centered on identifying the elements that are absent, all while failing to acknowledge that the most crucial absence is the embrace of the other person at the initial stage of our interaction. The beginning of the relationship is a total acceptance phase where we accept the other person as it is. Indeed, our system is not exempted from influence, and there exist certain elements that diverge from our system. Consequently, our efforts are likewise exerted with increased strength. However, should an individual conscientiously assume the responsibility and take a firm stance in order to effect change within the relationship, it is probable that your mutual bond will be revitalized. You will both undergo transformations and cease to remain unchanged. The elderly will depart, while the fresh will make their entrance. The forthcoming change will bring forth all aspects that are mutually pleasing to the partners, a fresh comprehension between the two individuals, and an illuminating perspective to perceive one's partner within the context of the relationship.

Imperfections are inevitable in any relationship as two individuals merge their distinct systems. However, when they demonstrate vulnerability without passing judgment upon one another, they are able to cultivate a flourishing relationship. Relationships can become strained when two individuals unite, endeavoring to impose their respective belief systems or perspectives upon one another. Nevertheless, it is imperative to transcend existing beliefs and discern the elements that harmoniously fortify the bond. The depth of the emotional connection ought to be intensified, a condition that can only be achieved within an environment devoid of judgment.

The subsequent contemplation entails a spiritual journey that will empower you to transcend the boundaries of acceptance and attain boundless self-realization. It will set you free on a systemic level as well as on the individual level and help you to look at your relationship in a new light where the level of understanding is a higher one. This novelty will facilitate a reinvigoration of your relationship, fostering increased affection, understanding, and fervor.

Shedding Negativity

You are angry. Your spouse departed from the premises earlier today, leaving behind a disorganized situation with the expectation that you would attend to it. He engages in this behavior each morning, evoking a sense of subservience within oneself. You perceive a sense of familiarity in being taken advantage of to the extent that it instigates a desire within you to separate from your spouse. However, due to a lack of self-assurance, you are unable to take any decisive action or vocalize your sentiments regarding the gradual erosion of your self-worth perpetrated by those around you. Your children engage in identical behavior. They fail to appreciate your contributions. They indiscriminately place their soiled footwear within the corridor, where you devoted an entire day to diligently sanitizing the flooring, without exhibiting the slightest concern for the sacrifices you made in order to assist them in their personal growth and development.

Stop right there!

In the course of one's existence, there are occurrences that evoke feelings of anger and resentment. The issue lies in your incomplete perception of the situation. You harbor feelings of resentment due to the manner in which individuals have been treating you. You have assumed the role of a passive recipient, but was it ever requested of you to willingly position yourself as a surface for others to tread upon? The issue at hand is that our perception of truth and the actual truth itself are divergent. If one perceives their life in a pessimistic manner, it will persist as their enduring reality, as it aligns with their subjective perspective.

It is probable that if you were to depart from your spouse and embark on a new path, you would discover that life persistently presents challenges as a means of demonstrating its effect on you. You compile all the available evidence. You compartmentalize these emotions within the confines of your consciousness, and subsequently, they give rise to feelings of resentment. Resentment inhibits one from perceiving the broader perspective, given its profoundly negative and spiritually demoralizing nature.

Please direct your attention to the quote provided at the outset of this chapter. Khalil Gibran effectively articulates the self-evident. According to the author's statement, we have the ability to select both our sources of happiness and distress, albeit to a certain degree. The pessimist will always see the darker side of any situation. Conversely, the individual who harbors a positive outlook will consistently perceive the favorable aspects of any given circumstance. Additionally, there is the matter of perceiving the cup as being either half empty or half full. Meditation enables individuals to perceive it as being half full and relinquish any feelings of resentment. Resentment affects everything. It eats into you. It renders one's life devoid of value. One must rid oneself of negativity to perceive the true purpose intended by one's divine creator upon one's arrival to this world. It is permissible for you to contend that you lack a deity, and that is also acceptable, as one does not necessarily require religious beliefs to derive benefits from the practice of meditation. The sole conviction that requires confirmation is the conviction in the present moment and your own abilities, and the practice of meditation offers you the opportunity to cultivate this belief.

Exercise in replacing negativity

A Buddhist monk positions himself outside the temple, depending upon the benevolence of individuals to procure sustenance for his nourishment. It's an established practice. He does not express thoughts such as 'I possess the desire for chicken today' or 'I am unable to consume additional servings of rice.' He has acquired, through the practice of meditation, the understanding that pessimistic ruminations hold no intrinsic value. They contribute no substance to his comprehension. Indeed, they would significantly impair his well-being. When Gautama Buddha embarked upon his retreat to the wilderness and assumed a posture beneath a tree, his ultimate objective was the discovery of a philosophical doctrine capable of alleviating human suffering. It was a prolonged process for him to come to the realization that it is the individuals comprising society who bear the accountability for their own discontent. As a result, he formulated a comprehensive modus operandi for existence that catered to their every desire for happiness. That does not pertain to meditation, yet it holds significance. When harboring negative thoughts, one diminishes their own potential and falls short of becoming the best version of themselves. When one displays anger, it is usually the person exhibiting the anger who experiences greater consequences than the recipient of their anger. When experiencing anxiety, one tends to endure an excessive amount of distress due to the heightened susceptibility to negative emotions, thereby exacerbating the anxiety.

Now, my objective is to help you become acclimated to substituting negative thoughts. This is justified by a valid rationale, as it forms an integral aspect of the practice of meditation. In the event that an individual engages in meditation while experiencing anger, distress, or a significant amount of negativity within their thoughts, it is probable that their meditation practice will be restricted, as their mind will frequently drift towards negative aspects. Therefore, acquiring the skill to substitute negative elements with positive ones represents a commendable strategy in order to engage in pre-meditation effectively, thereby enhancing your readiness for a productive meditation session. On subsequent occasions, whenever a negative thought arises, promptly substitute it with a positive one.

- Negative: I am increasingly discontented with individuals dictating my actions.
- Affirmative: Individuals perceive me as being significant and integral to their existence
- Adverse: The facial creases contribute to my aged appearance
Positive: The wrinkles on my countenance bear testament to the journey I have traversed.
- Negative: I am frustrated due to the children's failure to follow instructions.
- Affirmative: My offspring possess autonomous dispositions.

In this world, negative aspects are invariably accompanied by positive aspects. It is imperative that you strive to achieve a more equitable distribution of the resources. If one tends to adopt a generally pessimistic outlook or harbors a perception that life has treated them unfairly, it is imperative to consider a fundamental shift in one's cognitive framework. Maintaining a negative mindset will inevitably lead to a negative existence. The discovery of positivity in one's life enhances the capacity to effectively navigate adversities that arise therein. On a daily basis, you endeavor to make modifications in order to enhance your personal character. This does not imply an individual who harbors judgement towards others. It does not imply an individual with superior moral principles compared to others. Indeed, there is no requirement for comparison. The practice of meditation cultivates personal growth, fostering inner harmony among one's mind, spirit, and body, ultimately resulting in a more refined and integrated individual.

www.ingramcontent.com/pod-product-compliance
Lightning Source LLC
Chambersburg PA
CBHW050238120526
44590CB00016B/2132